To my no-longer-new babies, Emma and Wyatt,
and to their daddy, Erik, with love.
—H. M.

For Lee and Sally and their babies.
—L. R.

What to Expect When the New Baby Comes Home
Text and illustrations copyright © 2001 by Heidi Murkoff
What to Expect Kids™, Growing Up Just Got Easier™, and Angus™ are trademarks of Heidi Murkoff.
HarperCollins®, ▪®, and HarperFestival® are registered trademarks of HarperCollins Publishers Inc.
Printed in the U.S.A. All rights reserved.
Library of Congress catalog card number: 00-104552
www.harperchildrens.com

What to Expect
When the New Baby
Comes Home

Heidi Murkoff
Illustrated by Laura Rader

HarperFestival®
A Division of HarperCollins Publishers

A Word to Parents

The nursery's repainted, the layette's laid out, the infant car seat's standing by at the front door. The moment you've spent the last nine months preparing for is about to arrive, and with it a whole set of changes to the dynamics of your family life that you will probably never be *completely* prepared for.

As veteran parents (been there, done that, lived to tell about it), chances are you're a lot less anxious about bringing this newest addition home than you were about bringing home the first. No more needless fears about "breaking" the baby at changing time, about feeding too much or too little, about caring for the umbilical stump, about shampooing the soft spot.

Your child, however, won't have the benefit of experience when the new baby arrives. As a first-time sibling making that difficult shift from only child to older child, he or she will have plenty of questions (and, probably, a certain amount of anxiety) about what life with a newborn will be like.

How to prepare your child? *What to Expect When the New Baby Comes Home* is a good place to start. It will serve as a new-baby primer, giving your child the lowdown on these strange, wrinkled creatures, explaining exactly what new babies look like, what and how they eat, why they cry and demand so much attention, what they've done to deserve so many presents, when they'll walk and talk and become fun companions. This book will answer your child's many questions about new babies and will address some of the worries your child may have about sharing the house and your love with this mysterious newcomer.

In preparing a soon-to-be older sibling, try to paint as true a picture of what life with a new baby will and won't be like. Avoid unrealistic projections: that a new baby will be someone to play with (newborns can't play); that a new baby will be fun to have around (newborns don't do much more than eat, sleep, and cry); that life with a new baby will be the same as before (there will be times when the needs of a colicky baby will supersede those of an older sibling).

Of course, even the most thoroughly (and realistically) prepared child won't necessarily welcome the new baby with open arms. Virtually every older sibling experiences some feelings of jealousy, resentment, and even animosity, not just toward the new arrival, but also toward Mommy and Daddy (who spend so much time with the new baby). All of these feelings (whether they surface right away or in the months to come) are as normal as they are inevitable. They're also completely understandable. Encouraging your child to express these feelings (through words, dramatic play, pictures) rather than repress them will help resolve them faster. For instance, instead of censoring a refrain of "Let's send the baby back" or invalidating the feelings behind it ("You don't mean that—you love the baby!"), try to respond with empathy ("I know it's hard when the baby cries so much. Why don't we get him to sleep, so we can read a book together?").

Your actions will, as always, speak even louder than your words. Especially during this sensitive time, when so much time and attention are necessarily being devoted to the new baby, make sure your older child gets his or her fair share, too. Make feeding time story time; feed the baby cuddled up with your older child and a book. Use part of baby's naptime to play a favorite game. And whenever possible, divide and conquer: Dad stays home with the new baby, Mom goes to the park with the older child, or vice versa.

You'll notice that I have help explaining to your child what to expect when the new baby comes home. Because learning should be fun, too, I've created Angus, a lovable dog who provides answers to questions about growing up. Angus serves as a best friend and confidante throughout all of the What to Expect Kids™ books. He's a "transitional object" who will hold your child's hand as he or she faces new—and sometimes challenging—experiences.

For more tips on preparing your child for the arrival of a new baby, see *What to Expect the First Year* and *What to Expect the Toddler Years.*

Wishing you much happiness as new baby makes four (or more)....

Heidi

Just Ask Angus

Hello! My name is Angus. Some people call me the Answer Dog, because I like to answer all kinds of questions about growing up. It's good to ask questions because what you know, helps you grow!

So, I hear you have a new baby in your house, or maybe a new baby is coming to your house soon. Congratulations! That means you are (or are going to be) a big brother or sister—and a big brother or sister is a very special thing to be. It also means that your family is getting bigger and there are going to be a lot of changes at your house.

You and your mommy and daddy are probably pretty excited about the new baby, but I bet you have a lot of questions, too—questions about what new babies look like, what they do and don't do, and what having one around the house will really be like. I'm here to help—just ask me!

Are you ready to find out what to expect when a new baby comes home and what you can do to help? Then let's get started! Follow me. . . .

Your friend,

 Angus

P.S. I've put a little game or idea to think about on the bottom of every page. Look for my paw print, and you'll find it! Have fun!

What do new babies look like?

New babies don't look a lot like babies you see on TV or in books. They're really, really little, even littler than you might think. Just take a look!

Ask your mommy or daddy to show you some of the clothes you used to wear when you were a brand-new baby.

New babies' legs aren't straight like yours. Instead they are usually all curled up from spending so much time scrunched inside of Mommy's belly.

New babies have tiny toes!

New babies have a lot of wrinkles in their skin. Once they grow a little, the wrinkles will disappear.

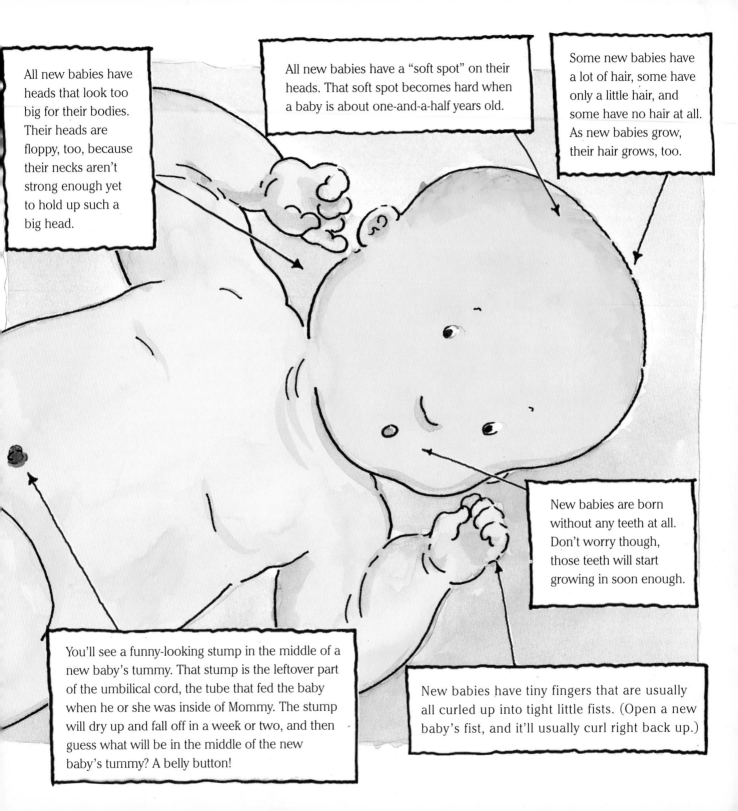

All new babies have heads that look too big for their bodies. Their heads are floppy, too, because their necks aren't strong enough yet to hold up such a big head.

All new babies have a "soft spot" on their heads. That soft spot becomes hard when a baby is about one-and-a-half years old.

Some new babies have a lot of hair, some have only a little hair, and some have no hair at all. As new babies grow, their hair grows, too.

New babies are born without any teeth at all. Don't worry though, those teeth will start growing in soon enough.

You'll see a funny-looking stump in the middle of a new baby's tummy. That stump is the leftover part of the umbilical cord, the tube that fed the baby when he or she was inside of Mommy. The stump will dry up and fall off in a week or two, and then guess what will be in the middle of the new baby's tummy? A belly button!

New babies have tiny fingers that are usually all curled up into tight little fists. (Open a new baby's fist, and it'll usually curl right back up.)

What do new babies eat?

New babies eat only one food, and actually, they don't eat it at all—they drink it. Can you guess what it is? That's right, milk. But they don't drink the kind of milk you have in your refrigerator. The milk they drink is a special milk that's just right for new babies. It looks more watery and tastes a little strange to anyone who isn't a new baby. Mommies can make this special milk in their breasts, and new babies can drink it right from their mommy's nipples. That's called nursing or breast-feeding. Or mommies can buy this special milk and put it in bottles for their new babies to drink. That's called bottle-feeding. Some new babies just bottle-feed, some new babies just nurse, and some new babies do both. Ask your mommy or daddy which way you ate when you were a new baby.

New babies sometimes swallow air when they drink, and that air makes bubbles in their tummies that can hurt. Babies need help pushing the air out. That's called burping. Practice burping your doll or stuffed animal. Hold it on your shoulder, and rub or pat it gently on the back. *Burp!*

> A gentle pat on the back will help a baby burp.

Why do new babies cry so much?

New babies can't talk yet, like you can. They can't use words to say, "Mommy, I want breakfast," or "Daddy, will you play with me?" The only way they have of telling their mommies and daddies what they need is to cry, which is why they cry a lot. New babies cry for many different reasons. They may cry because they're hungry or sleepy, because they're bored or need a cuddle, because something hurts or they're too hot or too cold, or because they have a wet or dirty diaper. Usually Mommy or Daddy can figure out why the new baby is crying, and they can help make the crying stop. All that crying can sometimes be hard to listen to, and you may get pretty tired of hearing it. But don't worry. Once the new baby learns how to talk, he or she won't have to cry so much.

Most babies say their first word sometime around their first birthday. Ask Mommy or Daddy what your first word was and how old you were when you said it.

My first word was "bone"! What was your first word?

Some Reasons Why New Babies Cry

Mommy

new baby

They're hungry

crib

cozy blanket

They're sleepy

Daddy

diaper cream

clean diaper

They need a clean diaper

New babies cry a lot, but they don't have tears until they're about a month old.

Angus

Why do new babies eat and sleep so much?

New babies have very tiny tummies that fill up quickly and empty out quickly. That's why they have to eat so much more often than you do—as often as twelve times a day or more. (That's like having four breakfasts, four lunches, and four dinners, all in the same day!) In fact, the only thing that new babies do more than eat is sleep. New babies are really small when they're born, but they grow really fast. All that growing is hard work, and it makes new babies very tired, so they need to sleep a lot. But they don't do a lot of sleeping all at one time, like you do. Instead, they sleep for a little while, then eat (to fill that tiny tummy!), then sleep some more, and eat some more—all day and all night. As babies get older, they start to sleep longer at nighttime and stay awake longer during the day. They also stop eating so often!

Let's read this book quietly, so the baby won't wake up!

New babies take lots and lots of naps during the day. When the new baby is sleeping is a good time for quiet time. What's your favorite thing to do during quiet time?

Why can't new babies do anything by themselves?

When there's a new baby in the house, it may seem like Mommy and Daddy are always busy taking care of him or her. That's because when new babies are born, they don't know how to do very much by themselves (besides cry!). They can't walk or crawl, so they need to be carried around. They can't dress themselves, so they need to be dressed. They can't feed themselves, so they need to be fed. They can't wash themselves, so they need to be washed. They can't use the potty, so they need their diapers changed (a lot!). Little by little, as they get bigger and bigger, new babies learn how to do more and more things by themselves, just like you did. And guess who can help the new baby in your house learn all those things—you can!

Think of all the things you've learned to do since you were a new baby. Ask Mommy or Daddy to write them down, and you can draw pictures. Look how long the list is!

Why do new babies have to be held so much?

When new babies are born, they've just finished spending nine months (which is almost a whole year) inside their mommy's belly. New babies are used to being warm, snug, and cozy, and that's why being held and cuddled makes them so happy. (And keeping new babies happy is good, because when they're happy, they don't cry as much!) But guess what new babies like even more than being held—being held and rocked. Rocking makes new babies feel calm and peaceful, and it usually helps them fall asleep. And when the new baby falls asleep, whose turn will it be to be held? Yours!

New babies can't hold their heads up by themselves because their necks aren't strong enough yet.

New babies like to be held snugly with their heads resting on an arm. Learning how to hold a new baby the right way takes practice. Practice holding your doll or stuffed animal snugly in your arms. Then ask Mommy or Daddy to help you hold the new baby.

Can I help take care of the new baby?

Taking care of a new baby is a lot of work, and there are plenty of things you can do to help. You can hand your mommy or daddy the diapers and the diaper wipes when it's time to change the baby (maybe you can help close the diaper, too). You can keep the baby busy by making funny faces when it's time for a shampoo (babies don't usually like shampoos). You can give the baby a pacifier or sing a soothing song when he or she is crying. You can be extra quiet when the baby's trying to fall asleep (whisper, whisper, whisper), and you can let Mommy or Daddy know when the baby wakes up. Some of the new-baby care—like rocking and feeding—has to be done by grown-ups. That's okay, because you can rock and feed your stuffed animal or doll at the same time!

Sometimes you may get tired of all the time Mommy and Daddy spend taking care of the new baby. When that happens, think of something special you can do with your mommy or daddy when the baby is sleeping!

Can I play with the new baby?

It's really easy to play with a new baby if you remember three rules. One, always, always be gentle. Two, only play with the new baby when there is a grown-up in the room. Three, you can't play with a new baby the same way you play with friends your own age, at least not yet. New babies are still too small to throw a ball or put together a puzzle. Here are some ideas for playing with the new baby: You can sing or dance for the new baby. You can talk to the baby in different voices (squeaky, soft, high, low) and see what the baby seems to like best. Or you can hold up a rattle or a soft toy for the baby to look at (new babies can't hold a toy by themselves). But do you know what game the new baby will think is most fun of all? Watching you, no matter what you're doing!

You'll be surprised how tightly the new baby can hold your finger!

Here's a game you can play with the new baby. Open the baby's palm and tickle it. The baby won't laugh (new babies aren't ticklish yet, and they don't know how to laugh). But he or she *will* grab your finger really tight.

Why do new babies get so many presents?

When a baby is born, it's a very special time. It means that there's a brand-new member of your family—a new child for Mommy and Daddy and a new brother or sister for you. That's exciting for everyone: grandmas and grandpas, uncles and aunts, cousins and friends. To welcome the new baby into your family, many of these people will bring or send presents like clothes, toys, or books. (People gave you presents when you were born, and I bet you probably still have some of them!) New babies are too little to open presents by themselves. Maybe you can open some of the presents for the new baby at your house and show him or her what's inside!

The nicest present can be one you make for the new baby. Draw a picture and ask Mommy or Daddy to put it on the baby's wall next to the crib or changing table. That's one of the best ways of all to welcome the new baby!

That's beautiful! What a special gift for the new baby!

When will the new baby be as big as me?

Looking at a new baby, you'll find it hard to believe he or she will ever be as big as you are. But new babies do grow fast. By the time the new baby is six months old, he or she will probably be big enough to sit up and start eating baby food. When the new baby is a year old, he or she will probably be big enough to walk. Not long after that, the new baby will be big enough to talk, and run, and climb, and draw, and do many of the other things you do. In fact, you can probably teach the baby to do a lot of these things as he or she grows up. But do you know what? Even when the baby gets big, you will always be a big brother or sister—a very special person to be in a very special family like yours. Hooray for you!

How many people were in your family before the new baby arrived? How many people are in your family now?

Can you count how many people are in your family?